Dear God...

Prayers for Children

David Haas

Dear God...

Prayers for Children

Illustrations by Monique Thouin Kantor

A Crossroad Book
The Crossroad Publishing Company

1997
The Crossroad Publishing Company
370 Lexington Avenue, New York, NY 10017

Illustrations by Monique Thouin Kantor
Designed by The Kantor Group, Inc., Minneapolis, MN
Author photo by Rick Norton/Norton Photostock

Printed in Canada

Library of Congress Catalog Card Number: 96-72494

ISBN: 0-8245-1656-7 (pbk.)

Contents

Going to Bed

Dear God,

Going to bed is never exactly the same –

sometimes I'm really tired

and like it when bedtime comes.

But sometimes,

most of the time,

I don't want to go to bed.

I hate it sometimes when Mom and Dad

make me go to bed.

I feel like I'm **missing out**

on some of the fun that they are having.

I want to stay up,

and be with them.

Sometimes I don't like being a kid,

and this can sometimes be one of those times.

Sometime I don't like going to bed

because I feel scared.

Sometimes I am scared of the dark.

Sometimes I am scared

because I don't like to be alone.

Sometimes I am scared

because I am afraid that I might not wake up.

Help me to not be **afraid,**

and remember that you are with me.

Even though I cannot see you,

I can talk to you.

And if I listen closely,

I can hear your voice

in my head and in my heart.

Then I feel safe.

God, with your help

I can be okay with going to bed now,

and feel safe to fall asleep

and dream the dreams

you have in store for me.

Help me to sleep well,

have good dreams,

and wake up happy for a new day.

Good night, God —

and may you have good dreams, too.

Amen.

Good Morning

Dear God,

Thank you for waking me up today,

and thank you

for the dreams I had —

even the ones that I do not understand.

I feel rested and ready

for the wonderful day you have planned for me.

I'm excited about the things I know

will happen today.

I'm excited (but also a bit scared)

about the **surprises** that will happen today.

Help me to be ready,

help me to pay attention

so that I will be able to handle

whatever happens.

Help me, God,

Help me to be **good to everyone**

I am with today:

my parents, the members of my family,

my teachers and my friends.

Help me especially to think well of

and be good to those people

who do not like me very much.

It is hard,

but I know you want me to be like you,

and be good to everyone.

Help me to always be thankful.

Help me to always remember

not to take this day for granted,

and to remember that every day

is a **wonderful day** because you made it so.

Help me to be a good person today.

God, I hope you have a good day too.

Amen.

When I am Mad

Dear God,

Right now I am really mad!

Someone hurt me

and treated me badly,

and right now,

I want to hurt them right back!

I know you do not like it when people

are mad at one another,

but I can't help it.

I'm mad!

Other people keep telling me

that I have to get over it

and be forgiving.

But it does not seem fair!

I want them to forgive me first.

After all,

they started it.

But then I remember

how your Son, Jesus,

was to those who were mean

to him.

They hurt him,

made fun of him,

and even killed him.

And even though those people

did those terrible things to him,

he forgave them,

and he asked you to forgive them.

I suppose if Jesus can forgive,

I guess I can, too.

I have to remember that he forgives me

when I treat others badly,

over and over again

even when I forget to ask for forgiveness.

It is still hard.

I still feel mad.

God, I don't want to just say "I'm sorry"

and not mean it.

Help me to really feel it,

and if I am not ready to say

"I forgive you" to another person,

to be okay with waiting

until I do feel like forgiving.

Help me to be more like Jesus,

to honestly be forgiving,

to not just say the words,

but mean it with my whole heart.

Thank you, God.

Thank you for letting me feel these feelings.

If I am not ready to forgive right now,

I will keep praying to you,

hoping that you will help me.

It's okay that I feel mad.

It's okay that I do not feel ready yet.

It's not okay though,
if I don't try hard to **keep working**
on wanting to forgive.

I will get back to you, God.

Don't give up on me.

It will get easier to forgive soon.

Amen.

When I am Scared

Dear God,

I get really scared sometimes.

In fact,

I am scared right now.

I do not know how to say what I am feeling,

I feel **strange** inside.

Help me, God,

help me to remember

that I am not alone.

Help me to remember

that you are with me,

and you know why I feel scared.

Please,

hold me close right now,

help me to feel better,

help me to be sure

that whatever is scaring me right now

will go away.

Please stay with me

until the fear goes away.

You are my friend, God,

my best friend.

Whatever does happen,

you will go through it with me.

That helps a lot.

Thanks.

Amen.

I'm So Happy

Dear God,

I am so happy!

I am glad, too,

because I do not always feel this way.

But when I do,

well,

it's just unbelievable –

it is just the **best** thing there is!

Sometimes I am happy

for a reason,

and that may be why I am happy right now.

And other times I'm happy,

and I do not even know why!

I may be feeling that way now.

When I feel this way, God,

I am hoping that you are happy today too.

I also hope that my parents, my family,

and all my friends are happy as well.

Everyone deserves to feel the way I do right now!

Help me to remember this feeling

when things are not going so well,

_{when} I feel sad,

and when I feel as though nothing is going right.

It is those times, God,

when I need to remember days like today.

I hope that I have more happy days

than sad days.

Knowing that you are in my life, God,

I have a good chance.

Don't you agree?

God, thanks for helping me to be happy.

Amen.

I Am Sorry

Dear God,

I messed up,

and I feel awful.

I wish it would have never happened –
I wish I could go back and fix it.

I didn't mean to hurt this person,

or do anything bad.

I don't know why it happened,

I am confused.

I am really, really sad for the wrong

that I have done.

I don't want you to be disappointed in me.

I sure feel **disappointed in myself.**

Right now I feel as though I don't deserve

to have you love me.

God,

you know everything about me,

and you know everything I have done –

good and bad.

You know that I feel sorry,

and that I will try to never do it again.

Please help me to not feel bad

about myself.

For I know you will never leave me,

and never stop loving me.

Help me to love myself right now.

It is hard.

Thanks for hanging in there with me

and for giving me another chance at things.

Next time I will try to **do better.**

Thanks for loving me, God,

no matter what I do.

Amen.

When I Miss Someone

Dear God,

I don't understand sometimes

why people whom I love

have to be far away from me.

When I am with these people,

    I feel great,

        I feel wonderful,

            and I feel like a whole person.

Then one of these people leaves –

they move away,

get married,

or for some reason they can't see me anymore,

or the **very worst,**

they die.

God,

there are times that I miss certain people so much!
I feel that way now.

You know how sad I am right now,
and I know you feel sad for me.

Please God,
take care of these people whom I miss so much,
help them to be happy.

Most of all,
help me to remember
that even though these people may be gone from me,
they are still around,
and there are wonderful memories that I can remember,
and gifts and objects
that keep me close to them.

Bless these people, God.

Help me remember everything good about them,

and how much I miss them.

It is the best way I can love them.

Thank you, God,

thank you for giving me

the sometimes painful feeling of missing someone.

Amen.

Thank You, God

Dear God,

There is so much to be thankful for,

I do not even know where to begin!

I thank you for so many wonderful things:

for this beautiful world,

for the **beautiful** things I see all around me:

for the rain and snow,

for the sun and the moon,

for all the different times of the day.

I thank you for the ability to learn more,

and for the ability to think and not be confused.

I thank you that I am the way I am,

no matter how that may be!

Even if I cannot see or walk,

even if I do not have some of the same things

that others have,

I still thank you – because I have what I have!

And what I have is all I need!

Thank you for my family,

and for all the people in my life who love me,

who take care of me,

and all who think I am wonderful and special!

I thank you for music and for dancing,

and for all beautiful things!

I thank you even for the things that are hard:

when someone dies whom I love,

when I am hurt by someone,

when I feel sad,

and when I feel scared.

I thank you for these things, too,

because these are the things that remind me

and all of us

that **we are alive!**

There is so much to be thankful for,

and I do not understand how some people

do not believe in you.

How could there not be a God?

How could you not be there?

How could you not be you?

I know you are real,

and I **thank you so much.**

Thank you, God.

Amen.

When I Am
In Trouble

Dear God,

I'm in trouble again.

I don't know what is wrong with me,

I try very hard not to mess up,

and to behave well and not make mistakes.

And now, I have to face the fact

that I may be punished.

Every time this happens I say to myself

that I will never let it happen again.

And it still happens.

I'm so mad at myself.

God, help me to remember

that no matter what I do,

no matter how badly I may behave,

you will always love me.

But also help me to remember,

that just because you always forgive me –

it does not mean that I should not try hard

to be as good as I can be.

I want you to do more than just forgive me.

I also want you to be **proud of me.**

Help me not to be mad at myself,

and help me to remember

that if you forgive me,

I should forgive me, too.

Thank you, God.

Amen.

Who Are You, God?

Dear God,

It is so hard sometimes to imagine

what you are really like.

I see a lot of pictures and paintings

by people who **think they know**

what you look like.

Sometimes you look really old,

with a long, white beard,

and you have deep,

almost scary looking eyes.

I close my eyes sometimes

and try to imagine what you look like.

Sometimes I think that

the way I think you really are is not

always the same way in which I have been taught.

Sometimes you are a woman,

sometimes you have **different** colored skin,

sometimes you are young,

and sometimes you seem

just like me.

I pray many prayers

    that others have written to you.

        Some of the prayers make you seem

            very far away.

I see all of the beautiful things around me,

the water and the trees,

the sun and the rain,

and I think,

wow, you can do some really neat things!

And then,

there are times that I do not understand you at all.

I am told that you guide

everything that happens in our lives,

and some of the things do not make sense at all.

I do not understand why people

sometimes are hurt,

and why people get sick and die.

I do not understand why people

have to fight with one another.

I do not understand why we have war,

and why so many people are hungry,

and why people hate and hurt one another.

Everyone tells me that you are a loving God.

How can that be,

when these bad things always seem to happen?

Who are you?

Even though I do not understand

everything that you do,

I keep on thinking that you are smarter than I am,

and that there is a reason for these things.

And while a lot of sad things happen,

there are so many wonderful things

that must be from you as well.

They seem to be the things

that are around me all of the time:

my wonderful family,

my friends,

and the fact that I keep waking up each day.

These are good things,

things that I feel so thankful for.

Who are you, God?

You are more than just the pictures

that I have seen.

You are my best friend,

and the one thing that I can always count on.

I do not need to know everything about you,

I just need to **believe in you.**

I want you to know that I do.

Thanks for letting me talk to you

and let you know what I am thinking.

Amen.

Going to Church

Dear God,

I do not always understand

why people go to church.

I mean,

if you are everywhere,

and if you are in my heart,

why do I have to go to **another place**

to find out where you are?

Sometimes people say that when

we go to church,

we are going to your house.

It seems as though you have a lot of houses,

because some of my friends

go to other places to be with you.

You also seem to like different kinds of houses,

because when we go on vacation

or when we visit Grandpa and Grandma,

it seems that none of the houses are the same.

Sometimes they are big or small.

The people sing different songs at some of these places,

and sometimes the prayers are different.

And its strange,

because not everyone seems to agree about you.

Sometimes I like going to church,

and other times I hate it.

Sometimes it's boring,

and I know it is,

because I see other people around

me who seem bored, too.

I guess your house is a lot like my house.

Sometimes being at home with my parents

and my family is fun and exciting,

and other times it is dull and not much fun.

Sometimes I am happy there,

and other times I am not.

I guess going to church is not that much different.

Maybe that is what you are trying to tell me –

maybe you are trying to teach us

that just because we believe in you and love you,

it does not mean that things are always fun and happy.

Maybe you're trying to teach us

that we go to church not to run away from our lives,

but we go to church so we can remember

that **you are always with us**.

Maybe you are helping us to understand

that you want us to try hard

not to forget you,

to remember that all of the good things we have

are because of you.

And maybe you're also trying to help us realize

that the sad things that happen

are much like some of the sad things

that happened to Jesus.

Jesus had a hard life -

and yet he was able to be happy in the end.

Maybe that is why we go to church,

to remember what Jesus had to go through,

and we have to go through some of the same things,

and that it will be okay.

I am glad I have a church that I can go to.

Thanks God.

Amen.

Birthdays

Dear God,

I love birthdays!

Do you know why?

Of course you do,

but I want to tell you anyway.

The most **important reason**

that I love birthdays so much,

is because it seems that people

try to be good to each other on birthdays.

They seem especially good to the birthday person.

When My Mind Wanders

Dear God,

It is hard for me to always pay attention.

And when I don't,

I often get into trouble.

Sometimes I miss something

the teacher says,

or something my Mom tells me,

or I think about other things at the same time.

When I pray to you I sometimes get distracted, too.

I have to remember that I am not perfect,

I am not like you,

nor should I try to be.

You never wander away from me,

even though sometimes I think you do.

When I think that way,

I have to remember that it is because

I am wandering, not you.

I have to be kinder to myself.

After all, God,

I'm only **human.**

Of course you know that,

but I often forget.

Help me not to wander off too much.

But also help me to remember that you forgive me

when I do.

I love you, God.

Thanks for loving me.

Amen.

I Have A Problem, God

Dear God,

I need your help,

and I am not sure what to do.

You know what my problem is, God,

because you know everything.

I am **feeling really anxious,**

and my stomach feels all strange inside.

I do not know how to help it feel better.

Do you have some advice for me?

Let me just be quiet for a few moments.

Maybe that will help.

(I'll take a few moments to **be still** if I can)

Thank you God for listening to me.

Even though I don't know exactly what to do right now,

I know that I will figure things out.

And I know that you will help me,

like you have before.

I'll keep you posted God on how I am doing,

and I know you will be there for me.

Thanks a lot, God.

Amen.

My Friends

Dear God,

Thank you for my friends.

I really like them.

I feel sorry for people I know

who don't seem to have any friends.

I cannot imagine what that would be like.

I also want to thank you, God,

for loving my friends

just like you love me.

I know you want us to **be happy**

and to enjoy being with each other.

Most of the time I do enjoy being with my friends,

though sometimes we fight and don't get along.

When that happens,

I feel bad,

and I try hard to become friends with them again.

Most of the time it works.

It helps me to realize how special it is to have friends.

It is not always easy to be a good friend.

Sometimes being a friend means having to do things

that the other person wants to do,

even if I do not want to do it.

I know that my best friends are the ones

who think about what makes me happy.

Help me to be a **good friend**, God.

Just like you are to me.

Thanks for being my friend.

Amen.

When Someone Dies

Dear God,

I feel as if I cannot stop crying.

I feel so sad,

Why do people have to die?

I feel alone right now.

This is hard for me to understand.

God, you know how bad I feel.

What will my life be like now?

Why do we have to die?

I guess these feelings are okay,

because Jesus cried too

when his friend Lazarus died.

He loved him very much.

But I have to admit, God,

these sad feelings are really painful.

God, will you please wipe away my tears?

Will you please hold me and love me right now?

I really need you.

Please stay with me, God,

until I feel better.

Thanks.

Amen.

Taking A Trip

Dear God,

I am really excited!

I am so lucky to be able

to travel and see things

that I have never seen before.

Every trip is a **new adventure**,

even if I am going somewhere

I have been before.

I sometimes forget that many of my friends

are not as lucky,

and that some of them never get to go

any place.

No matter how close or how far I may go,

there are wonderful things to see and do.

Sometimes the way there is fun, too,

being able to go in the car,

or **fly on a plane,**

and sometimes by train or by boat!

No matter how we are going,

or where we are going,

I ask you God,

to keep all of us safe.

Help us to have the best time,

to get along with each other,

and most of all,

keep me awake and aware of everything we do.

Come with us, God!

We'll have a great time!

Amen.

Being Alone

Dear God,

sometimes I hate being all by myself.

Right now, I am alone,

and I don't like it at all.

Sometimes when I am alone I feel **forgotten,**

by my parents,

    or by my friends,

        and sometimes,

            I feel you are far away, too.

Sometimes just being in my body

does not feel like enough.

I feel better when others arc around –

members of my family,

or my friends,

with a lot of activity,

a lot of talking and playing,

lots of people around.

But right now,

it feels very **very strange,**

and I am really scared.

Do you ever feel lonely, God?

I wonder sometimes.

I mean,

we are always praying to you,

and it seems we pray to you only when

we need your help,

but not just to talk.

Who do you talk to when you feel lonely?

Maybe we can help each other out.

Let's talk to one another often,

especially when we are alone.

And when we do that,

we will forget that we are all by ourselves,

because we won't be alone any more,

we will be **with each other.**

Be with me now God,

and I will try to be with you.

Together,

I bet it will not be so scary.

Amen.

Laughter

Dear God,

I love to laugh!

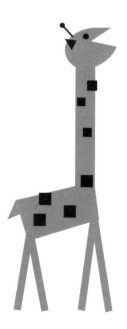

When I laugh,

I forget my troubles,

and I know that when I

make someone else laugh,

they feel better, too.

Sometimes I laugh and laugh

so hard,

I start to cry and my stomach hurts!

Laughter must be one of the greatest

things you have given us,

and it seems to be one of the best things

we can ever do.

To help make someone smile and laugh

is one of the most **important things**

we can try to do for each other.

I know there are a lot of people who

do not have much to laugh or smile about.

Why am I so lucky?

I know you want everyone to be happy,

to smile and laugh,

but for some people,

something seems to get in the way.

God, I pray for **all people**

who need to laugh,

and all those who seem to be sad.

Help me to remember

that you want them to laugh,

and if there is anything I can do

to help,

I will.

I love to laugh, God.

When I do,

I feel you are inside of me,

and I know that you are smiling.

Thank you, God.

Amen.

When I
Have Lied

Dear God,

my insides do not feel good at all.

I told a lie,

and I really **feel bad** about it,

and I do not know what to do.

I mean,

no one got hurt.

Except me.

I hope you're not disappointed in me.

I feel like I just could not tell the truth,

because I did not want to get into trouble.

But now I feel that I am in deeper trouble,

because it is hard to keep the lie secret,

and it is hard to not feel bad.

And of course,

I know that you know the truth

no matter how clever I might be.

Whenever I lie,

and whenever I have to admit it later,

I feel even worse.

God,

help me to be strong enough

to admit that I lied,

and help me to never do it again.

When I tell the truth,

I always feel closer to you

and **happier with myself.**

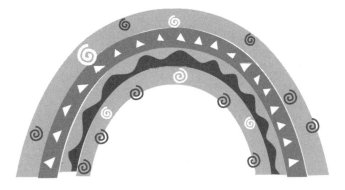

I know that no matter what,

you will always love me.

So one of the best ways

for me to thank you,

is to tell the truth. Always.

Amen.

I'm Hungry

Dear God,

I'm hungry!

It is so great to wake up each morning

and have breakfast!

Lunch is great too!

And it is **wonderful** to have dinner,

especially dessert!

There are so many wonderful things

to eat,

to taste and drink,

and I have so many favorite foods,

and there are some things that I have to eat,

that I don't like.

But that's okay,

because that makes the better food even better!

Sometimes we go out to eat,

but I like **eating at home** the most!

God, when I do not eat all of the food

on my plate,

sometimes the grownups talk about

children in parts of the world far away,

or even close by —

who have nothing to eat.

I cannot imagine not having food!

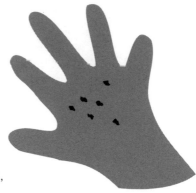

Why is it, God,

that I have enough food to eat,

and at the same time,

some kids have **nothing to eat at all?**

I can't figure it out.

I mean,

you must love them too, don't you?

God,

I feel sorry for them.

Please help them,

and help me and all of the children

and grownups find ways to feed

those who are hungry.

Help the farmers grow enough food

for all to share,

and help people to find ways to

find all of those who are hungry,

and give them food to eat,

so they can grow strong and happy like me.

Most importantly, God,

help me to always be **thankful**

for all that you have given to me.

Thanks God.

Amen.

A New Baby
Is Here

Dear God,

a new baby is here!

It is amazing to realize

that I was once that small,

and everybody looked at me

the same way they are now looking

at this new baby.

The hands and fingers are so small,

and the baby is almost bald!

Wow! It's like magic –

Babies seem to come from nowhere.

Ever since this new baby has come,

I feel like everybody pays more attention

now to the baby then they do to me.

I hope they have not **forgotten me.**

But I have to remember,

that all babies come from you,

and they come from Mom and Dad

loving each other very much.

I am here for the same reason!

And they love me too,

just like you do!

But right now, because this baby is so small,

and not as grown up as I am,

it needs more help than I do right now.

The baby needs my help, too,

especially when it grows up,

but even right now.

When I look into those little eyes,

and feel those tiny little fingers around mine,

help me to remember that you, God,

look at us the same way,

with the same feeling of "wow,"

and the same love

that is in our family right now.

I guess that means that no matter

how much I grow,

I will always need to be your child

and have you hold me in your arms.

Thank you for our lives, God.

Amen.